INVENTION FACT FRENZY!

by Cari Meister

CAPSTONE PRESS
a capstone imprint

Published by Capstone Press, an imprint of Capstone
1710 Roe Crest Drive, North Mankato, Minnesota 56003
capstonepub.com

Invention Fact Frenzy! was originally published as *Totally Amazing Facts About Outrageous Inventions*, copyright 2017 by Capstone Press.

Copyright © 2026 by Capstone. All rights reserved. No part of this publication may be reproduced in whole or in part, or stored in a retrieval system, or transmitted in any form or by any means, electronic, mechanical, photocopying, recording, or otherwise, without written permission of the publisher.

Library of Congress Cataloging-in-Publication Data is available
on the Library of Congress website.

ISBN: 9798875233845 (hardcover)
ISBN: 9798875233791 (paperback)
ISBN: 9798875233807 (ebook PDF)

Summary: There's an INVENTION FACT FRENZY headed your way! Did you know that inventor Thomas Edison held more than 2,000 patents? Or that the first submarine was a rowboat covered in leather? Even a budding young inventor is sure to learn something surprising as they flip through these pages.

Editorial Credits
Editor: Ali Deering; Designer: Jaime Willems; Media Researcher: Svetlana Zhurkin; Production Specialist: Whitney Schaefer

Image Credits
Alamy: Imaginechina Limited, 27 (top), Smith Archive, 54; Associated Press: Paul Sakuma, 56; Bridgeman Images: Photo © Boltin Picture Library, 23 (bottom), Prismatic Picture, 46; Getty Images: -Oxford-, 15, Archive Photos/Pictorial Parade, 53, Authenticated News, 41 (top), Bettmann, 55 (top), 62, 63, Express, 39 (middle), Fotosearch, 48, FPG Intl., 12, gadost (skateboards), cover, back cover, General Photographic Agency, 32 (top), Gwengoat, 9 (top), Hulton Archive, 8 (top), 16, 38, 42, 45 (middle), Hulton Archive/Fox Photos/Norman Smith, 61 (middle), Hulton Archive/Topical Press Agency, 60, Michael Ochs Archives, 44, Vladi333, 9 (bottom), WireImage/Bob Riha Jr, 20, Yvonne Hemsey, 57; Library of Congress: 18, 19; Newscom: Album/Walt Disney Pictures/Pixar Animation Studios, 33; Shutterstock: Alano Design, 31, Artsiom P, 25, Brad Whitsitt, cover (top right), Brothers klia, 8 (bottom), CkyBe (speech bubbles), cover and throughout, Crevis, 59 (bottom), Ekaterina_Minaeva, 49, enter89, 4 (right), Everett Collection, 5 (top), 14, Fordham Dabney, cover (top left), 64, Gavran333, 34 (top), gentle studio, 47 (bottom), glenda, 13 (right), gn8 (rays and lines), cover and throughout, goir, 52, Gojindbefs, 29 (top), Gopal3366, 45 (bottom), Guppic the duck, cover (funny accessories), h3c7orC, 1 (top), 37, igra.design, 4 (middle), James Steidl, 4 (left), Javier Jaime, 26, 28, Lana Brow, 34 (middle), Lana Nikova (gears), cover and throughout, lantapix, 24 (top), leolintang, 24 (middle), Lewis Tse, 51 (middle), Luba Vega, 61 (top), Lumella, 50, Massimo Parisi, 40, Massimo Todaro, 7, Md. Sykhul Islam Shamim (clouds), 36, 37, mikeledray, 47 (top), Nor Gal, 6 (bottom), Ntguilty, 6 (top), oasisamuel, 21, oneinchpunch, 35, PhotoVrStudio, cover (bottom left), 10 (top), Pranch, 17 (top), Rasulov, 30, Ratheesh Mohan NML, 23 (top), Rawpixel, 13 (left), Roman Samborskyi, 5 (bottom), 41 (bottom), Senimanto_ID, 27 (bottom), Sinhyu Photographer, 58, SN VFX, 10 (bottom), SooperYela, 32 (bottom), SpiceVectors, 51 (top), Stanislav-Z, 11, Steve Mann, 39 (top), Tetiana Chernykova, 17 (bottom), The Mariner 4291, 29 (middle), v_kulieva (gradient background), back cover and throughout, Westermak, 43, WH_Pics, 22, WhiteDragon, 59 (top), Yuliya Chsherbakova, 55 (bottom); Smithsonian Institution: National Museum of American History, 1 (bottom); SuperStock: Mary Evans Picture Library/Pantheon, 36

Any additional websites and resources referenced in this book are not maintained, authorized, or sponsored by Capstone. All product and company names are trademarks™ or registered® holders of their respective holders.

Printed and bound in the USA. PO 6307

Table of Contents

An Incredible Collection of
Invention Facts 4

Legendary Inventors 6

Famous Firsts 22

Historic Inventions..................................... 36

Wacky Inventions 54

AN INCREDIBLE COLLECTION OF INVENTION FACTS

Have you ever stopped to wonder exactly WHY something was invented? For example, did you know the first use of wheels wasn't for transportation? Or maybe you want to know important things like how many LEGO® Minifigures have been made. (Hint: It's a lot!) Or you might be curious about the first computer-animated movie. Well, lucky for you, we have the answers. And all *you* have to do is read this book to learn them. If you're ready to uncover these answers and more, turn the page for a frenzy of invention facts.

LEGENDARY INVENTORS

Archimedes lived from 287–212 BC.

Archimedes invented a pump to draw water uphill. It is known as the Archimedes' screw.

Archimedes also invented weapons of war. His Claw of Archimedes was a huge hook that could flip enemy ships.

Leonardo da Vinci lived from 1452–1519.

Da Vinci painted the famous *Mona Lisa*. But he also designed flying machines, tanks, and scuba suits.

Da Vinci used mirror writing, meaning he wrote from right to left. Did he do this to keep people from stealing his ideas or to keep the ink from smearing? No one knows.

Galileo lived from 1564–1642.

With his telescope, Galileo discovered four of Jupiter's moons.

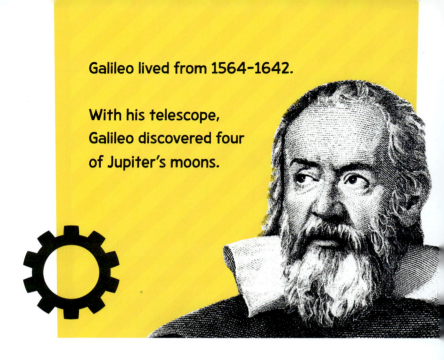

Galileo proved Copernicus's idea that the planets go around the sun.

Galileo also invented the first pendulum clock, but he never quite finished it.

Benjamin Franklin lived from 1706-1790.

Franklin's inventions include bifocals and the rocking chair. He also invented the Franklin stove and the lightning rod.

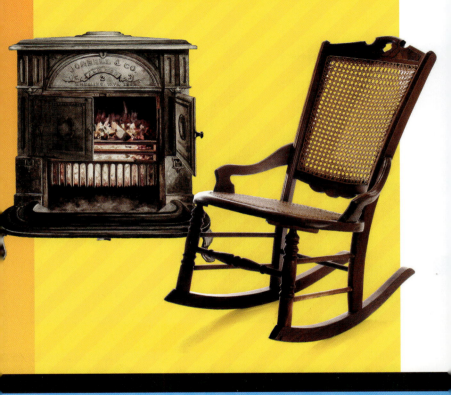

Franklin almost died while trying to heal a paralyzed man by electrocuting him.

Thomas Edison lived from 1847–1931.

WOW!

THOMAS EDISON HAD A TOTAL OF 2,332 PATENTS WORLDWIDE.

Thomas Edison invented thousands of things, including the phonograph, the universal electric motor, the incandescent light bulb, and the movie camera.

The first message recorded on Edison's phonograph was "Mary had a little lamb."

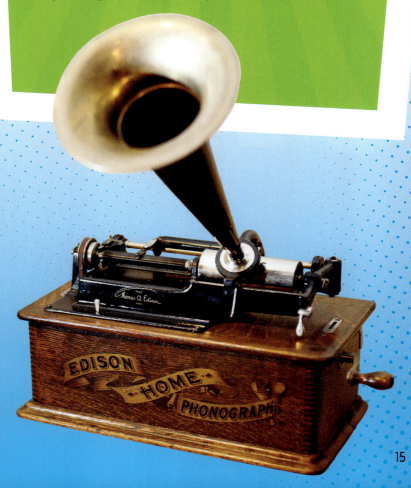

George Washington Carver lived from 1864–1943.

Contrary to popular belief, Carver did not invent peanut butter. The Aztecs and Incas were the first known peoples to mash peanuts into a paste and spread it on food.

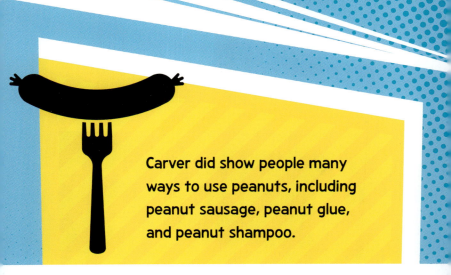

Carver did show people many ways to use peanuts, including peanut sausage, peanut glue, and peanut shampoo.

Wilbur Wright lived from 1867–1912.
His brother Orville lived from 1871–1948.

WILBUR (LEFT) AND ORVILLE (RIGHT)

The Wright brothers invented the first heavier-than-air powered aircraft. It was called the *Wright Flyer*.

In 1903, the Wright brothers' first flight lasted only 12 seconds.

Frank Zamboni lived from 1901–1988.

In 1953, Zamboni patented the first "ice resurfacer."

Zamboni's company also invented The Grasshopper—a machine that rolls out Astroturf™—and The Black Widow—a machine that puts dirt on top of graves.

FAMOUS FIRSTS

The first wheel was invented around 3500 BC. It was used to make pottery.

Three hundred years later, wheels were put on carts.

The first wheels in North America were used on children's toys.

The Chinese were the first people to use rockets. They used them for fireworks.

The rockets that took men to the moon were more than 363 feet (111 meters) tall.

Space shuttles from NASA—the National Aeronautics and Space Administration—had solid rocket boosters that could go to full power in only two-tenths of a second. It takes longer to blink your eyes!

Hero of Alexandria invented the first vending machine 2,000 years ago. It gave out holy water.

In 1883, Percival Everitt invented a machine that gave out postcards.

IN CHINA AND JAPAN, PEOPLE CAN BUY LIVE CRABS FROM A VENDING MACHINE.

The first working submarine was a rowboat covered in leather.

The Turtle was the first submarine used in battle. It was meant to attach bombs to ships, but it failed.

How deep do today's United States submarines go? That's classified information!

Sir John Harington invented the first flush toilet in 1596.

Today's toilets use up to 1.6 gallons (6.1 liters) of water per flush. Until the mid-1990s, they used up to 7 gallons (26.5 l).

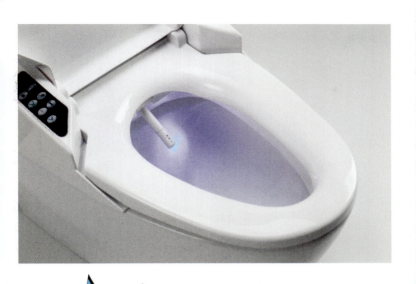

WOW!

SOME HIGH-TECH TOILETS CLEAN THEMSELVES AND CLEAN (AND DRY) YOU TOO! THEY ALSO HAVE HEATED SEATS, SOUND SYSTEMS, AIR FRESHENERS, AND NIGHT-LIGHTS!

The Apostle (1917) was the first animated feature film. No copies exist today.

WALT DISNEY

Many early cartoon characters, including Mickey Mouse, had only four fingers. They were easier to draw that way.

Toy Story (1995) was the first feature film animated entirely by computer.

In the 1950s, the first skateboard was made by attaching roller skate wheels to a board.

Hermosa Beach, California, was the site of the first-ever skateboarding contest in 1963.

The skateboarding "bowl" came about because of California droughts. Pools were emptied, and skateboarders used them to do new tricks.

HISTORIC INVENTIONS

In 1783, Louis-Sebastien Lenormand made a parachute out of two umbrellas and jumped from a tree.

In 1797, a French prisoner held in a tall tower designed the first high-altitude parachute. Upon his release, he tested it by jumping from a balloon 3,200 feet (975 m) in the air. He lived!

Da Vinci's parachute design from the 1400s was tested in 2000. It worked! And it had a smoother ride than today's parachutes.

The earliest cameras were big and clunky. Models had to sit totally still for one to three minutes or the photos blurred.

The first camera widely used by the public was the Brownie. It came out in 1900 and cost $1.

The Polaroid, or instant picture camera, went on sale in 1948. The camera held special paper and chemicals inside. Photos could be taken and printed within 60 seconds.

In 1837, Charles Babbage built an early computer called the "Analytical Machine."

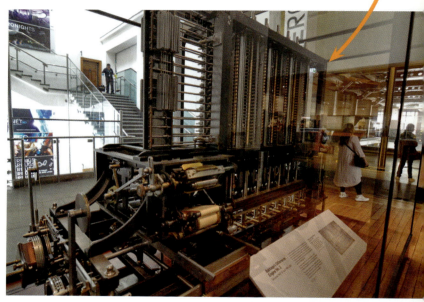

Early computers were so big that they filled entire rooms!

Today's smartphones have more processing power than those large computers had.

French inventor Nicolas Cugnot built the first car in 1769. It was powered by a steam engine.

Cugnot's car didn't go very fast. Its top speed was about 2.5 miles (4 kilometers) per hour!

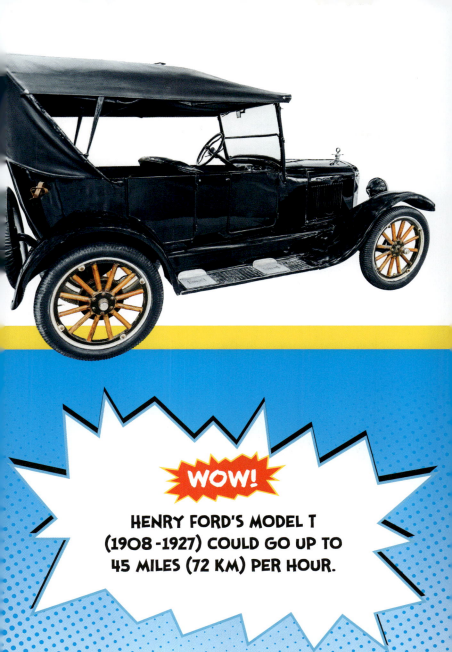

WOW!

HENRY FORD'S MODEL T (1908-1927) COULD GO UP TO 45 MILES (72 KM) PER HOUR.

Mary Anderson invented windshield wipers in 1903.

Anderson's first wipers were made of wood and rubber. She attached them to a lever near the vehicle's steering wheel.

Car companies thought wipers were useless and turned down Anderson's idea. Her patent ran out, and she never made a dime on her invention.

Ten years later, windshield wipers were standard on cars.

Alexander Graham Bell is widely thought to be the inventor of the telephone. He made his first call in 1876.

Levi Strauss and Jacob Davis invented jeans in 1873. They were first invented as sturdy work pants for miners.

Rivets were put in jeans so the seams did not tear.

WOW!

JEANS FIRST CAME IN ONLY TWO COLORS: BLUE AND BROWN.

Ole Kirch Christiansen began making and selling wooden LEGO® toys in 1932. The first plastic bricks were sold in 1949.

THE LEGO® MOLDS ARE VERY EXACT. ONLY ABOUT 18 IN EVERY ONE MILLION PIECES ARE THROWN AWAY FOR POOR QUALITY.

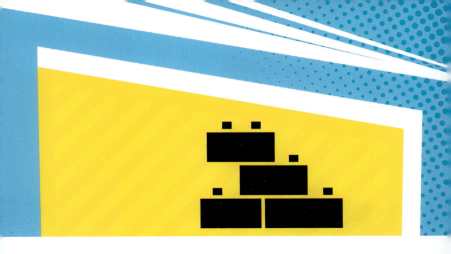

More than four billion LEGO® Minifigures have been made. That's nearly three times the population of China!

The microwave oven was invented by accident during World War II.

While Percy Lebaron Spencer was using a radar, he noticed his candy bar had melted nearby. The radar worked by using micro waves. This discovery led to cooking foods with micro waves.

The first microwave oven weighed about 750 pounds (340 kilograms). It stood nearly 6 feet (1.8 m) tall.

WACKY INVENTIONS

In 1936, Isabella Gilbert invented the Dimple Maker.

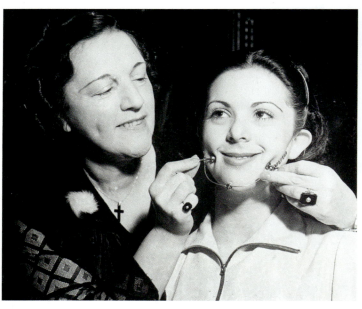

ISABELLA GILBERT (LEFT)

Gilbert's device had a spring with two small knobs that fit over a person's face. The knobs pressed into the cheeks.

Did the Dimple Maker work? Not really.

In 1984, Timothy G. Zell "made" unicorns by performing surgery on the horn buds of white baby goats.

Some of the "unicorns" were sold to Ringling Bros. and Barnum & Bailey Circus.

Dr. Alpheus Myers invented a tape worm trap in 1854.

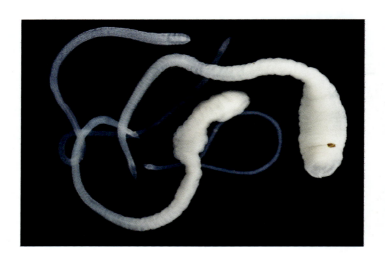

How did the trap work? After fasting for several days, the patient swallowed a baited trap attached to string. When the tapeworm found the bait, the trap shut and grabbed the tapeworm's head.

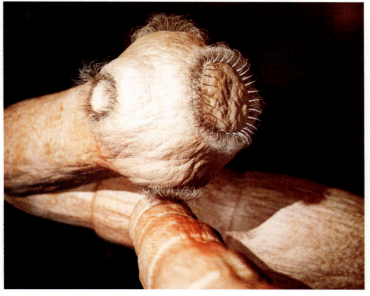

The patient then pulled on the string, bringing the tapeworm up and out.

Emma Read invented a baby cage in 1922. The idea was that babies who lived in apartments needed fresh air and sun too.

The wire cage hung on the side of a building, outside an open window. Some cages had a roof to protect babies from rain and snow.

Hugo Gernsback invented the Isolator in 1925.

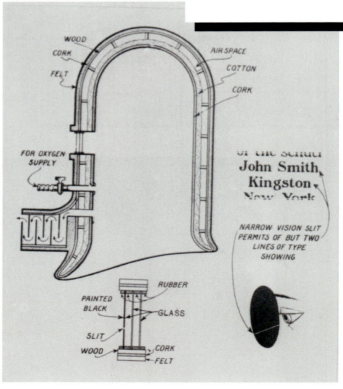

People who wore the Isolator could hear nothing and see very little. It isolated them, allowing them to concentrate better on the task at hand.

The Isolator had an oxygen tank because it could get a little stuffy in there!

BOOKS IN THIS SERIES

   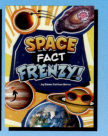